CHRISTINE HAGGINS

Prayers for Personal Growth and Transformation

Embrace Change, Discover Purpose, and Unlock Your Full Potential

Contents

INTRODUCTION

Welcome to "Prayers for Personal Growth and Transformation: Embrace Change, Discover Purpose, and Unlock Your Full Potential." Within the pages of this book, you will embark on a journey of spiritual exploration and self-discovery, guided by the power of prayer.

In our lives, we often encounter seasons of change, both expected and unexpected. It is during these times that we may feel uncertain, overwhelmed, or even fearful. Yet, through prayer, we can find solace, strength, and a deep sense of peace, knowing that we are not alone in our struggles. Prayer connects us with the divine presence of God, who walks with us through every step of our journey.

This collection of prayers has been carefully curated to address the core themes of personal growth and transformation. Whether you are standing at the threshold of change, seeking purpose and direction, or longing to unlock your full potential, these prayers will serve as a source of inspiration, encouragement, and guidance.

Within these pages, you will discover prayers that embrace change as an opportunity for growth. They will help you find the strength and courage to navigate the unknown, to release what no longer serves you, and to embrace the transformative power of God's love and grace.

Additionally, this book will guide you in discerning your purpose and aligning your life with God's divine plan. Through prayers of discernment, you will be encouraged to listen attentively to the gentle whispers of your heart and to seek God's guidance in uncovering the unique gifts and talents He has bestowed upon you. You will be inspired to live a life of meaning and significance, using your abilities to make a positive impact on the world around you.

Furthermore, these prayers will nurture your faith, deepen your trust in God, and empower you to unlock your full potential. As you delve into the pages of this book, you will be invited to cultivate a deeper relationship with the Divine, to embrace self-compassion, and to embark on a journey of spiritual growth that will transform your life from the inside out.

May these prayers serve as a constant reminder that you are loved, cherished, and called to live a life of purpose. As you immerse yourself in prayer, may you experience the transformative power of God's presence, guiding you to embrace change, discover your purpose, and unlock the boundless potential within you.

May this book be a source of comfort, inspiration, and encouragement as you navigate the twists and turns of your personal journey. May it ignite a fire within your heart, fueling your desire to grow, transform, and live a life that radiates God's love and light.

May these prayers be a catalyst for personal growth and transformation in your life, as you open your heart to the divine possibilities that await you.

May your journey through this book deepen your faith, illuminate your path, and empower you to embrace change, discover your purpose, and unlock your full potential.

May these prayers be a companion and a guide as you embark on this sacred quest of personal growth and transformation.

Welcome to a world of prayer that will change your life.

COMPANION GUIDE

x

As you journey through the different prayers in this book, you might want to keep a journal close to pen down revelations and personal request.

This Prayer Request Journal specifically tailored for this purpose is all you need.

SCAN ME

I

Embracing Change

Chapter 1: Finding Strength in Times of Change

Prayer for Embracing Change

Dear Heavenly Father,

In the midst of the shifting seasons of life, I come before You with an open heart and a willingness to embrace change. Help me to release my grip on the familiar and step into the unknown with confidence and trust. Fill me with a spirit of adaptability and resilience, knowing that You are my constant anchor in the midst of change.

Grant me the wisdom to recognize the opportunities that lie within transitions. May I view change as a catalyst for growth, a chance to shed old limitations, and a doorway to new possibilities. Help me to see beyond the temporary discomfort and envision the beauty that awaits on the other side of change.

As I navigate through this transformative journey, guide my steps and reassure me of Your unwavering presence. Remind me that You are the God of all seasons, the One who orchestrates change for my ultimate good. Strengthen my faith, that I may trust in Your divine plan, even when it seems uncertain or challenging.

I surrender my fears, doubts, and resistance to change into Your loving hands. Fill me with Your peace that surpasses all understanding, anchoring my soul as I embark on this new chapter of my life. Grant me the grace to embrace change with grace, courage, and unwavering trust in Your unfailing love.

In Jesus' name, I pray. Amen.

Prayer for Courage in Transition

Heavenly Father,

In the midst of this season of transition, I come before You, seeking Your strength and courage. Change can be intimidating and unsettling, stirring up a whirlwind of emotions within me. But I know that You have called me to walk through this journey with courage and unwavering faith.

Grant me the boldness to face the unknown and the resilience to overcome any obstacles that may come my way. Help me to let go of the fear that holds me back, and instead, embrace this transition as an opportunity for growth and transformation.

When doubt creeps in and uncertainty clouds my mind, remind me of Your promises. Reassure me that You are always with me, guiding and protecting me every step of the way. Give me the courage to take bold leaps of faith, knowing that You are my steady rock and my unfailing support.

Fill my heart with confidence, knowing that You have equipped me with everything I need to navigate this transition. Help me to embrace the challenges as stepping stones toward becoming the person You have created me to be. May Your Spirit empower me, giving me the courage to face each new day with hope and determination.

I place my trust in You, Heavenly Father. You are the source of my strength, and I know that in You, I can find the courage to navigate this transition with grace and resilience.

In Jesus' name, I pray. Amen.

Prayer for Trusting God's Plan

Loving Father,

As I stand at the crossroads of change, I humbly surrender my plans and aspirations into Your loving hands. You know the desires of my heart, and You have a purpose for every season of my life. Help me to trust in Your divine plan, even when it diverges from my own.

When uncertainty lingers and doubt creeps in, remind me that Your ways are higher than my ways. Your plans are perfect, and Your timing is impeccable. Give me the faith to believe that Your path for me is far greater than anything I could ever envision for myself.

When I face moments of confusion or feel lost in the midst of change, guide my steps and illuminate my path. Open my eyes to the signs and nudges that indicate Your presence and direction. Teach me to rely on Your wisdom and lean not on my own understanding.

As I journey through this season of change, grant me the grace to let go of control and surrender to Your divine guidance. Help me to release any resistance or fear that hinders my ability to trust You fully. Fill me with a deep sense of peace, knowing that You are always working for my good, even in the midst of uncertainty.

Lord, strengthen my faith in Your faithfulness. Remind me of the countless times You have provided, protected, and guided me throughout my life. Help me to recall Your faithfulness in times past, so that I may have confidence in Your faithfulness in the present and future.

When doubt and impatience arise within me, remind me of Your perfect timing. Give me the patience to wait for Your plans to unfold, knowing that Your timing is always perfect. Help me to embrace the journey and the lessons it holds, even when it doesn't align with my immediate desires or expectations.

I surrender my plans, dreams, and anxieties to You, dear Father. Help me to trust that You hold the blueprint of my life and that You will lead me on the path that is best for me. Fill me with a deep sense of peace as I relinquish my control and trust in Your sovereign will.

In the midst of change, may my trust in You deepen and my faith be strengthened. May I rely on Your unwavering love and wisdom to guide me through each step of this journey. Thank You for Your constant presence and Your steadfast commitment to my growth and well-being.

In the name of Jesus, I pray. Amen.

Chapter 2: Overcoming Challenges

Prayer for Perseverance

Heavenly Father,

In the face of challenges and adversity, I come before You, seeking Your strength and perseverance. Life's journey is filled with obstacles and trials that can sometimes feel insurmountable. But I know that with You by my side, I can overcome any challenge that comes my way.

Grant me the determination to press on when the path seems difficult and the road ahead appears long. Help me to keep my eyes fixed on You, knowing that You are my source of strength and my refuge in times of trouble. Fill me with a steadfast spirit, enabling me to rise above the challenges and emerge stronger than before.

When weariness threatens to consume me and discouragement tries to take hold, remind me of Your promises. Assure me that You are with me, guiding and sustaining me through every storm. Help me to trust in Your faithfulness and to rely on Your power, for in my weakness, Your strength is made perfect.

Give me the courage to face adversity with grace and resilience. Help me to learn from the challenges I encounter, allowing them to shape me into a person of greater character and compassion. May my struggles become stepping stones toward growth and transformation.

I surrender my fears, doubts, and limitations to You, Lord. I know that in You, I can find the strength to persevere. Grant me unwavering faith, unyielding determination, and unshakable hope. With You by my side, I can overcome any challenge and walk victoriously in Your love and grace.

In Jesus' name, I pray. Amen.

Prayer for Finding Peace in Difficult Times

Loving God,

In the midst of life's storms and difficult seasons, I

come before You, seeking Your peace that surpasses all understanding. The world around me may be filled with chaos, but within the depths of my soul, I long for the tranquility that can only be found in Your presence.

Grant me the serenity to accept the things I cannot change, the courage to change the things I can, and the wisdom to discern the difference. When the weight of life's challenges bears down on me, envelop me in Your loving arms and fill me with a sense of calm and peace.

Help me to surrender my worries, anxieties, and burdens to You, knowing that You are my ever-present help in times of trouble. Teach me to lean on Your promises and to find solace in Your Word. Guide my thoughts and emotions, that I may fix my gaze on You and not be overwhelmed by the storms that surround me.

In the midst of difficulties, grant me clarity of mind and a steadfast heart. Enable me to find rest in You, knowing that You are in control and working all things together for my good. May Your peace, which transcends all understanding, guard my heart and mind in Christ Jesus.

Fill me with Your peace, Lord, so that I may become a vessel of peace to those around me. Help me to extend compassion, kindness, and understanding, even in the midst of my own struggles. May Your peace shine through me as a beacon of hope to a world in need.

In the name of Jesus, I pray. Amen.

Prayer for Strength in Trials

Dear Heavenly Father,

In times of trials and tribulations, I turn to You, seeking Your strength and fortitude. Life's challenges can be overwhelming, and at times, it feels as if I am being tested beyond my limits. But I know that Your strength is made perfect in my weakness, and with You, I can endure and overcome.

Grant me the strength to persevere when the weight of adversity bears down on me. Help me to stand firm in the face of trials, knowing that You are my rock and my fortress. Fill me with Your power and might, empowering me to rise above the challenges that come my way.

When I feel weary and depleted, remind me of Your

promises. Assure me that You will never leave me nor forsake me, and that You are working all things together for my good. Strengthen my faith, that I may trust in Your unfailing love and unwavering faithfulness, even in the midst of trials.

Lord, when I face moments of doubt and discouragement, help me to turn to Your Word for encouragement and guidance. Grant me the wisdom to discern Your voice amidst the noise of the world, and the courage to follow Your leading.

In times of weakness, remind me that Your grace is sufficient. Help me to surrender my burdens to You, knowing that You are the One who carries my load and provides me with the strength I need. Teach me to rely on Your power and not my own, for in You, I find true strength.

I pray for the endurance and patience to persevere through the trials that come my way. Strengthen my character and deepen my faith as I walk through these challenging times. Help me to emerge stronger, wiser, and more compassionate.

Lord, I ask for Your strength to overcome every obstacle, to face adversity with courage, and to triumph over every trial. May my struggles become testimonies of Your faithfulness and Your ability to bring beauty from ashes.

Thank You for the promise of Your presence and Your unwavering support. In the midst of trials, I find solace in knowing that I am never alone, for You are always with me. Grant me the strength to endure, the wisdom to learn, and the faith to trust in Your plans.

In Jesus' name, I pray. Amen.

Chapter 3: Seeking Inner Transformation

Prayer for Renewal of Mind and Spirit

Heavenly Father,

I come before You, longing for a deep inner transformation. I desire to be renewed in mind and spirit, to be transformed into the person You have created me to be. Cleanse my thoughts, purify my heart, and restore my soul, O Lord.

I surrender my mind to You, asking for Your divine intervention. Remove any negative patterns of thinking, self-doubt, and limiting beliefs that hinder my growth. Fill my mind with thoughts that are pure, noble, and praiseworthy. Help me to fix my gaze on You, that my thoughts may align with Your truth and purpose for my life.

Renew my spirit, O Lord. Breathe new life into my weary soul and awaken within me a passion for Your presence. Fill me with Your Holy Spirit, that I may be empowered to live a life that glorifies You in all I do. Transform my desires, aligning them with Your will, that I may walk in obedience and experience the fullness of Your blessings.

Grant me the willingness to let go of old habits, attitudes, and mindsets that no longer serve me. Help me to embrace the process of renewal, even when it is uncomfortable or challenging. Strengthen me with Your grace, that I may persevere in seeking transformation from within.

As I immerse myself in prayer and meditation, open my eyes to the areas of my life that need transformation. Reveal to me the areas of my character that need refinement and the habits that need to be replaced. Help me to cooperate with Your Spirit as You mold me into the likeness of Your Son, Jesus Christ.

I surrender my mind, my thoughts, and my spirit to Your transformative work, dear Lord. Mold me, shape me, and make me new. May my inner transformation be a testimony of Your love, grace, and power at work in my life.

In Jesus' name, I pray. Amen.

Prayer for Letting Go and Surrendering

Loving Father,

I come before You, recognizing that true transformation begins with surrender. I acknowledge that there are areas of my life where I have held on tightly, afraid to release control. Today, I choose to surrender all to You, knowing that You have a perfect plan and purpose for my life.

Help me to let go of my own agendas, desires, and expectations. Teach me to trust in Your divine wisdom and timing. Grant me the courage to surrender my will to Yours, even when it feels uncomfortable or uncertain. May my surrender be an act of faith, acknowledging that You are the author and perfecter of my life.

I release my fears, my anxieties, and my need for control into Your loving hands. I trust that You will work all things together for my good, even when I cannot see the bigger picture. Help me to relinquish my grip on the things of this world and fix my eyes on the eternal.

In the process of surrender, grant me a heart of humility and submission. Help me to recognize that Your ways are higher than my ways and Your thoughts are higher than my thoughts. Align my will with Yours, that I may walk in obedience and experience the fullness of Your blessings.

Give me the grace to surrender my past, my mistakes, and my regrets to You. Heal my wounded heart and restore my soul. Help me to fully embrace the forgiveness and redemption You offer through Jesus Christ, that I may walk in the freedom of a surrendered life.

In the act of surrender, may I find true peace, con-tentment, and joy. May my life become a testament to the power of surrendering to Your will and Your ways. Use me as an instrument of Your love and grace, that others may witness the transformative power of surrendering to You.

Lord, I surrender my plans, my dreams, and my future into Your loving care. I trust that You have a perfect plan for me, one that far exceeds anything I could ever imagine. Help me to let go of my own limited understanding and embrace Your divine guidance.

In the process of surrender, I ask for Your strength to face the challenges that may arise. Grant me the faith to trust that You are working all things together for my good, even in moments of uncertainty. Help me to find peace in knowing that You are in control and that Your love for me is unwavering.

Teach me the beauty of surrendering my relationships to You. Help me to release any control or expectations I may have and allow Your love to flow through me. Grant me the wisdom to love others selflessly and to extend grace and forgiveness, just as You have done for me.

As I surrender to Your transformative work, I pray for a heart that is open and receptive to change. Grant me the courage to let go of old wounds, resentments, and bitterness. Fill me with Your healing and restoration, that I may experience the fullness of life in You.

Thank You, Lord, for the gift of surrender. I embrace it as an opportunity for growth, transformation, and deepening intimacy with You. May my surrendered life be a testimony of Your faithfulness and the abundant blessings that come from entrusting my all to You.

In Jesus' name, I pray. Amen.

Prayer for Inner Healing and Restoration

Dear Heavenly Father,

I come before You today, seeking Your divine intervention in the depths of my being. I acknowledge that there are wounds within me that need Your healing touch. I bring before You all the pain, hurt, and brokenness that I carry within my heart and soul.

Lord, You are the ultimate healer and restorer. I ask that You pour out Your love and grace upon me, and bring healing to the deepest parts of my being. Heal the wounds of past experiences, disappointments, and traumas. Mend the brokenness and restore the areas in my life that have been affected by pain and sorrow.

I surrender to Your healing power, knowing that You are the source of true restoration. I invite Your Holy Spirit to enter into the depths of my soul, bringing healing, peace, and wholeness. Remove any bitterness, resentment, or unforgiveness that may hinder my healing process. Replace it with Your divine love, forgiveness, and compassion.

Lord, I ask for the restoration of my identity and self-worth. Help me see myself through Your eyes, as a beloved child of God, fearfully and wonderfully made. Release me from any negative self-perception or destructive thought patterns. Fill me with Your truth and let it resonate deeply within me.

As I experience Your healing and restoration, help me to extend the same love and grace to others who may have caused me pain. Teach me to forgive and release them, just as You have forgiven and released me. Grant me the strength and wisdom to break free from the chains of the past and walk in the freedom of Your healing power.

I place my trust in You, knowing that Your plans for me are good, and that You desire my complete healing and restoration. May Your presence surround me and fill me with peace, joy, and a renewed sense of purpose. Let Your healing light shine upon me and bring forth the beauty that comes from being made whole in You.

I pray all these things in the precious name of Jesus, who bore our wounds and carried our sorrows, and through whom we find ultimate healing and restoration. Amen.

II

Discovering Purpose

Chapter 4: Discerning God's Will

Prayer for Seeking God's Guidance

Gracious Father,

I come before You with a humble heart, seeking Your divine guidance and wisdom. I acknowledge that Your plans for me are higher and greater than my own. Grant me the discernment to hear Your voice amidst the noise of the world and the clarity to understand Your will for my life.

As I embark on the journey of seeking Your guidance, quiet my spirit and open my ears to hear Your still, small voice. Speak to me through Your Word, through godly counsel, and through the gentle stirrings of Your Spirit within me. Help me to align my desires with Your desires and to surrender my will to Yours.

Guide me in every decision I need to make, whether big or small. Give me wisdom to choose the right path, even when it seems unclear or uncertain. Help me to trust that You will make my paths straight and lead me in the way everlasting.

Teach me to be patient, dear Lord, as I seek Your guidance. Help me to wait on You with expectancy and trust in Your perfect timing. Strengthen my faith to believe that You will reveal Your will to me when the time is right. May my seeking be characterized by faith, hope, and unwavering trust in Your faithfulness.

In the process of seeking Your guidance, guard my heart from doubt and confusion. Fill me with a peace that surpasses all understanding, knowing that You are in control and working all things together for my good. Help me to surrender my fears and anxieties to You, casting all my cares upon You, for You care for me.

I commit my plans, dreams, and aspirations to You, dear Father. Guide my steps and order my path according to Your will. May Your guidance be a lamp unto my feet and a light unto my path. As I seek Your guidance, may I walk in obedience and bring glory to Your name.

In Jesus' name, I pray. Amen.

Prayer for Clarity of Purpose

Dear Heavenly Father,

I come before You, seeking clarity of purpose and vision for my life. I desire to live a life that is aligned with Your will and brings honor to Your name. Illuminate my path and reveal to me the purpose for which You have created me.

In moments of uncertainty and confusion, grant me clarity of mind and heart. Remove any distractions or hindrances that cloud my understanding of Your purpose. Open my eyes to see the unique gifts, talents, and passions You have placed within me, and guide me to use them for Your glory.

Help me to discern the steps I need to take to fulfill Your purpose for my life. Give me the courage to step out in faith, even when the path seems unfamiliar or challenging. Grant me the wisdom to make decisions that align with Your purpose and the perseverance to stay the course, even in the face of obstacles.

Lord, I surrender my own desires and ambitions to You. Align my heart with Your heart and reshape my dreams according to Your divine plan. Transform my perspective, that I may view success not by worldly standards, but by the impact I can make for Your kingdom.

Fill me with passion and enthusiasm for the work You have called me to do. Grant me a deep sense of fulfillment and joy as I live out my purpose in service to You and others. Help me to make a difference in the lives of those around me, shining Your light and sharing Your love.

In the journey of discovering my purpose, may I find solace in Your presence. May I draw closer to You, seeking Your guidance and finding strength in Your unfailing love. Guide me, Lord, as I navigate the path that leads to fulfilling my purpose in You.

In Jesus' name, I pray.

Prayer for Openness to God's Direction

Gracious Lord,

I humbly come before You, recognizing that Your ways are higher than my ways and Your thoughts are higher than my thoughts. I surrender my own plans and ambitions, and I open my heart to receive

Your direction and guidance. Help me to be open and receptive to Your leading in every area of my life.

Lord, remove any pride, stubbornness, or self-will that may hinder me from hearing Your voice clearly. Soften my heart and make me sensitive to Your promptings. Give me a spirit of humility and teachability, that I may be willing to follow Your direction even when it challenges my comfort or understanding.

Grant me the discernment to distinguish Your voice from the many voices that surround me. Help me to tune out distractions and tune in to Your still, small voice speaking to my heart. Give me the courage to obey Your leading, even when it goes against the wisdom of the world or my own desires.

I surrender my plans and dreams to You, dear Lord. Help me to align my will with Yours and to trust in Your perfect timing. Fill me with patience and contentment as I wait for Your direction. Increase my faith to believe that You have a unique plan for my life and that Your timing is always perfect.

As I seek Your direction, guide my steps and order my path. Open doors that You want me to walk through and close doors that are not aligned with Your will.

Grant me the wisdom to make choices that honor You and bring about the fulfillment of Your purposes in my life.

Lord, I acknowledge that the journey of following Your direction may not always be easy. There may be challenges, uncertainties, and sacrifices along the way. But I trust that as I surrender to Your direction, You will provide the strength, grace, and resources I need to walk the path You have set before me.

Thank You, Lord, for Your faithfulness and Your promise to guide me. I place my trust in You and surrender my will to Your perfect plan. May my life be a testament to Your loving guidance and may I bring glory to Your name through my obedience.

In Jesus' name, I pray. Amen.

Chapter 5: Cultivating Gifts and Talents

Prayer for Discovering and Developing Gifts

Heavenly Father,

I come before You with a grateful heart, acknowledging that every good and perfect gift comes from You. Thank You for the unique gifts and talents You have bestowed upon me. I seek Your guidance in discovering and developing these gifts for Your glory and the benefit of others.

Grant me the wisdom to recognize the gifts You have placed within me. Open my eyes to see the areas where I excel and the talents that come naturally to me. Help me to understand how these gifts can be used to make a positive impact in the world and to further Your kingdom.

As I embark on the journey of discovering and developing my gifts, I pray for guidance and direction. Lead me to opportunities that will enable me to cultivate and refine these gifts. Surround me with mentors, teachers, and experiences that will nurture and challenge me to reach my full potential.

Teach me to be diligent and disciplined in honing my skills. Help me to invest time and effort into developing my gifts, knowing that they are entrusted to me for a purpose. Fill me with a hunger for knowledge and a desire to grow, that I may continually expand my abilities and use them to their fullest potential.

May I never boast in my own gifts, but instead humbly acknowledge that they are given to me by Your grace. Help me to use my gifts with humility, recognizing that they are meant to serve others and bring glory to Your name. May my actions and accomplishments point others to You, the ultimate Giver of gifts.

Lord, guide me in the discovery of new gifts that may be hidden within me. Help me to step out of my comfort zone and explore new areas of talent and creativity. Grant me the courage to embrace new challenges and the perseverance to overcome obstacles along the way.

May the development and use of my gifts be a source of joy, fulfillment, and purpose in my life. Use me, Lord, as an instrument of Your love and grace, utilizing the unique gifts You have bestowed upon me to bless others and bring about positive change in the world.

In Jesus' name, I pray. Amen.

Prayer for Using Talents to Serve Others

Loving Father,

I thank You for the talents and abilities You have entrusted to me. I recognize that these gifts are not meant to be kept for myself, but to be used for the benefit of others and for Your kingdom's purposes. Grant me the heart of a servant, eager to utilize my talents to serve and bless those around me.

Help me to identify the needs of others and to discern how my talents can be employed to meet those needs. Open my eyes to the opportunities that exist for me to make a difference in the lives of those who are hurting, broken, or in need of encouragement. Give me a spirit of compassion and empathy, that I may use my talents to bring healing, comfort, and hope.

Teach me to serve with humility, not seeking recognition or praise, but simply desiring to make a positive impact. Help me to use my talents selflessly, considering the needs of others above my own. Fill me with Your love and grace, that my service may be an expression of Your character.

Lord, grant me wisdom and discernment in how to effectively use my talents to serve others. Show me the areas where my gifts can have the greatest impact and where I can bring about positive change. Help me to use my talents responsibly and with integrity, always seeking to honor You and bring glory to Your name.

Guard me against pride or self-centeredness that may seek to hinder my service. Keep me focused on the needs of others and help me to be attentive to the leading of Your Holy Spirit. May my service be a reflection of Your love and a demonstration of Your kingdom here on earth.

As I use my talents to serve others, remind me of Your example of selfless service. Help me to follow in the footsteps of Jesus, who came not to be served but to serve. Fill me with His humility, compassion, and sacrificial love.

Lord, I pray for divine appointments and opportunities to serve those who are in need. Open doors for me to use my talents in ways that bring hope, joy, and encouragement to others. Guide me to the individuals, communities, and organizations that can benefit from my gifts, that I may be a vessel of Your love and grace.

May my service be characterized by kindness, generosity, and a genuine desire to uplift others. Help me to listen attentively, to empathize deeply, and to respond with wisdom and discernment. Use me as an instrument of Your peace, bringing comfort to the brokenhearted, strength to the weary, and support to those who are struggling.

Lord, I surrender my talents to You, knowing that they are ultimately Yours. I ask for Your guidance and direction in how to best utilize them for the greater good. Give me creative ideas and innovative solutions that can address the needs of others in meaningful ways.

Protect me from burnout or discouragement as I serve. Renew my strength and refresh my spirit, that I may continue to pour out Your love even when I feel weary. Remind me that my efforts, no matter how small, can make a significant impact in the lives of others.

May my service not be limited to acts of kindness alone but also extend to sharing the message of Your salvation and grace. Help me to use my talents as a platform to proclaim Your truth and to point others to the hope found in Jesus Christ.

Thank You, Lord, for the privilege of using my talents to serve others. May my life be a reflection of Your love and may Your name be glorified through my service. In Jesus' name, I pray. Amen.

Prayer for Wisdom in Utilizing Abilities

Gracious Father,

I come before You with a humble heart, acknowledging that every ability and talent I possess is a gift from You. You have entrusted me with these gifts, and I seek Your wisdom in utilizing them for Your glory and the betterment of others.

Lord, grant me discernment and understanding as I navigate the various opportunities and choices that lie before me. Help me to use my abilities in alignment with Your will and purpose. Give me the wisdom to discern where and how to invest my time, energy, and resources for the greatest impact.

Guide me in utilizing my abilities responsibly and ethically. Help me to be a good steward of the talents You have given me, using them with integrity and in ways that honor You. Guard me against selfish ambition or pride, and remind me that my abilities are meant to serve a greater purpose beyond my own desires.

Teach me to seek Your guidance in every decision I make. Grant me clarity of mind and an open heart to hear Your voice speaking to me. May Your Holy Spirit illuminate my path and lead me in the direction that aligns with Your plans for my life.

Lord, I surrender my abilities to You, acknowledging that they are not meant to be used solely for my own gain or recognition. Help me to use them to serve others selflessly and to bring about positive change in the world. Give me a heart of compassion and empathy, that I may use my abilities to uplift and empower those in need.

Grant me the courage to step out of my comfort zone and use my abilities in new and innovative ways. Expand my horizons and show me opportunities to make a difference that I may not have considered before. Help me to embrace challenges and overcome obstacles with perseverance and faith.

Lord, in moments of doubt or uncertainty, remind me that You have equipped me with the abilities I need to fulfill the purposes You have for my life. Help me to trust in Your provision and guidance, knowing that You will provide the resources and opportunities necessary for me to utilize my abilities for Your glory.

May my actions and the use of my abilities reflect Your love and grace. May they point others to Your goodness and draw them closer to You. May I be an instrument of Your transformative power, using my abilities to bring light, hope, and healing to a world in need.

Thank You, Lord, for the gifts and abilities You have given me. May I always seek Your wisdom in utilizing them and may Your name be glorified through my actions. In Jesus' name, I pray. Amen.

Chapter 6: Living a Meaningful Life

Prayer for Finding Purpose and Meaning

Gracious God,

I come before You with a longing in my heart to live a life of purpose and meaning. You have created me with unique gifts, passions, and dreams, and I seek Your guidance in discovering the purpose for which You have designed me.

Lord, in moments of confusion or uncertainty, I ask for Your clarity and direction. Open my eyes to see the path You have laid before me and grant me the wisdom to discern Your will. Help me to align my desires and aspirations with Your greater plan for my life.

Guide me in discovering my true calling, the work

that brings me fulfillment and allows me to make a meaningful impact in the lives of others. Show me how to use my talents, skills, and experiences to serve You and to contribute to the well-being of the world around me.

Lord, I surrender my ambitions and plans to You, knowing that You are the one who ultimately determines my purpose. Align my heart with Your purposes and grant me the courage to step out in faith, even when the path may seem uncertain or challenging.

Teach me to seek significance, not in worldly success or recognition, but in the knowledge that I am fulfilling the purpose for which You have created me. Help me to find joy and contentment in fulfilling Your will, even in the midst of trials and setbacks.

Lord, I pray for patience and perseverance on this journey of discovering and living out my purpose. Strengthen my faith and remind me that You are always with me, guiding and empowering me to fulfill the unique calling You have placed upon my life.

May my life be a testament to Your love and grace. Use me, Lord, as an instrument of Your peace and transformation in the lives of others. May my actions and words reflect Your character, and may others be inspired to seek their own purpose and meaning in You.

Thank You, Lord, for the gift of purpose. May I live each day with intention and passion, using my life to bring glory to Your name and to make a positive impact on the world around me. In Jesus' name, I pray. Amen.

Prayer for Impacting Lives with Love

Heavenly Father,

You are the source of all love, and You have called us to love one another as You have loved us. Today, I come before You with a desire to impact the lives of others with Your love. Fill my heart with Your compassion, empathy, and kindness.

Lord, teach me to see people through Your eyes, to recognize their worth and value, regardless of their background, circumstances, or beliefs. Help me to extend a hand of friendship, a listening ear, and a caring heart to those who are hurting, lonely, or in need of encouragement.

Grant me the ability to love others selflessly, without expecting anything in return. May Your love flow through me, touching the lives of those I encounter. Give me the wisdom to know how to meet the needs of others, whether through acts of service, words of affirmation, or simply being present with them in their struggles.

Help me to be a vessel of Your love in my family, my community, and beyond. Give me opportunities to demonstrate Your love through acts of kindness, forgiveness, and reconciliation. May my actions be a reflection of Your grace and may they bring hope and healing to those who are broken.

Lord, guard me against judgment and prejudice. Help me to embrace diversity and to treat all people with dignity and respect. Show me how to bridge divides, to promote understanding, and to foster unity in a world that is often divided.

Empower me, Lord, to make a difference in the lives of others. Use me as an instrument of Your love and mercy, that through me Your love may be experienced by those around me. Help me to be intentional in my words and actions, seeking opportunities to share Your love and to bring comfort, encouragement, and hope to those who are in need.

Lord, I pray for the wisdom to discern when someone is hurting or in need of a listening ear. Grant me the ability to offer genuine compassion and empathy, being present with others in their joys and sorrows. May Your love flow through me as I extend a helping hand, offer words of encouragement, or simply lend a supportive presence.

Teach me to be patient and understanding, recognizing that everyone carries their own burdens and struggles. Help me to extend grace and forgiveness, just as You have shown me. Guide me in cultivating relationships that are rooted in love and characterized by kindness, humility, and mutual respect.

Lord, use me as an agent of reconciliation and peace. Help me to navigate conflicts with wisdom and humility, seeking unity and understanding. May Your love empower me to break down walls of division and promote healing in broken relationships.

Remind me, Lord, that even small acts of love and kindness can have a profound impact on the lives of others. Grant me the courage to step out of my comfort zone, to reach out to those who are marginalized or forgotten, and to be a voice for the voiceless.

Thank You, Lord, for the privilege of impacting lives with Your love. May my life be a reflection of Your unconditional love, and may Your name be glorified through my actions. In Jesus' name, I pray. Amen.

Prayer for Living with Intention and Gratitude

Gracious God,

You have given me the gift of life, and I desire to live each day with intention and gratitude. Help me to embrace each moment as an opportunity to honor You and to make a positive impact on the world around me.

Lord, teach me to live intentionally, with a sense of purpose and focus. Guide me in setting priorities that align with Your will and values. Grant me the discipline to make choices that reflect my commitment to You and to the things that truly matter in life.

Help me to be present in the here and now, fully engaged in each moment. Free me from distractions and busyness that can steal my attention and rob me of the joy and blessings that surround me. Open my eyes to the beauty and wonder of Your creation, and fill my heart with gratitude for the abundant gifts

You have bestowed upon me.

Lord, remind me of the brevity of life and the importance of making each day count. Give me the courage to pursue my dreams, to take risks for the sake of Your kingdom, and to live boldly in faith. May I never settle for mediocrity or complacency, but strive to grow, learn, and make a positive impact in the lives of others.

Teach me to cultivate a heart of gratitude, Lord. Help me to recognize and appreciate the blessings, both big and small, that You pour into my life each day. May thankfulness be the foundation of my attitude, shaping my interactions with others and fostering a spirit of contentment and joy.

Lord, I surrender my plans, desires, and aspirations to You. May Your will be done in and through my life. Give me the strength and courage to surrender control, trusting that Your plans are greater and more beautiful than anything I could ever imagine.

Thank You, Lord, for the gift of life and the opportunity to live it with intention and gratitude. May I bring honor to Your name and inspire others to live their lives in a way that brings glory to You. In Jesus' name, I pray. Amen.

III

Unlocking Your Full Potential

Chapter 7: Strengthening Faith and Trust

Prayer for Deepening Faith

Heavenly Father,

I come before You with a sincere desire to deepen my faith in You. I acknowledge that faith is a gift from You, and I humbly ask for an increase in faith, that I may trust You more fully and rely on Your promises.

Lord, strengthen the foundations of my faith. Help me to anchor my belief in Your unchanging character, in Your love, grace, and faithfulness. Increase my understanding of Your Word, that I may find wisdom, guidance, and encouragement within its pages.

Grant me the courage to seek You wholeheartedly, to

surrender my doubts and fears at Your feet. Teach me to lean not on my own understanding but to trust in Your infinite wisdom and sovereignty. Increase my faith to believe in Your power to work miracles and to bring about the impossible.

Lord, when doubts arise or when circumstances challenge my faith, remind me of Your faithfulness throughout history and in my own life. Help me to recall the times You have provided, protected, and guided me. Strengthen my resolve to trust You, even when I cannot see the outcome.

Lead me deeper into intimacy with You, Lord. Cultivate within me a vibrant relationship with You through prayer, worship, and the study of Your Word. Help me to hear Your voice clearly, to discern Your will, and to follow Your leading with unwavering faith.

Lord, I surrender my doubts, fears, and uncertainties to You. Fill me with Your peace that surpasses all understanding. Help me to walk by faith and not by sight, knowing that You are with me every step of the way.

May my deepened faith be a testimony to Your goodness and grace. Use my life as a beacon of light, drawing others closer to You. May my unwavering trust in You inspire those around me to seek You and experience the depth of Your love and faithfulness.

Thank You, Lord, for the gift of faith. Strengthen it within me, that I may live a life that glorifies Your name. In Jesus' name, I pray. Amen.

Prayer for Trusting God's Timing

Gracious Lord,

I confess that often I struggle to trust Your perfect timing in my life. I am impatient and anxious, desiring things to happen according to my own plans and timetable. Today, I humbly come before You and surrender my impatience to Your loving care.

Help me, Lord, to embrace the truth that Your timing is always perfect. Teach me to rest in the assurance that You know what is best for me and that Your plans for my life far exceed my own understanding. Increase my trust in Your sovereignty, knowing that You work all things together for my good.

In moments of waiting and uncertainty, grant me patience and perseverance. Give me the strength to surrender my desires and expectations to You, trusting that Your plans are greater and more beautiful than anything I can envision. Help me to find peace in the waiting, knowing that You are at work behind the scenes.

Lord, when doubt and discouragement creep into my heart, remind me of Your faithfulness. Show me examples from Your Word and from my own life where You have proven Yourself trustworthy. Renew my hope and help me to fix my eyes on You, the Author and Finisher of my faith.

Teach me to find contentment in the present moment, even as I eagerly await the fulfillment of Your promises. Help me to use this time of waiting to grow in faith, to develop perseverance, and to deepen my relationship with You. May I seek Your presence and guidance daily, finding strength and encouragement in Your Word.

Lord, I surrender my need for control and my desire for immediate answers. Help me to relinquish my timeline to Your loving hands. Grant me the grace to trust Your divine wisdom and perfect timing. Fill me with peace and contentment as I wait upon You.

In the midst of waiting, Lord, grant me the strength

to focus on the present moment. Help me to embrace the lessons and blessings that come with the journey, rather than solely fixating on the destination. Open my eyes to the opportunities for growth, character development, and deepening faith that arise as I trust in Your timing.

Lord, increase my faith and confidence in Your promises. Remind me that Your plans are not hindered by delays or detours. Help me to remember that You are always working behind the scenes, orchestrating circumstances for my ultimate good and Your glory.

Give me the wisdom to discern the difference between my own desires and Your will. Grant me the patience to wait for Your perfect timing, knowing that what You have in store for me surpasses anything I could have imagined.

Father, I lay my worries and anxieties at Your feet. Help me to surrender control to You and trust that You are working all things together for my benefit. Teach me to rest in Your love, knowing that You are faithful and that Your timing is always purposeful.

May my trust in Your timing be a testament to Your faithfulness and goodness. Use my life as a testimony to others, showing them the beauty of waiting upon You. May they witness the peace and joy that come from surrendering to Your timing, and may it inspire them to trust You more deeply in their own lives.

Thank You, Lord, for Your perfect timing. Strengthen my trust in You, and may I find peace and contentment as I wait upon Your plans to unfold. In Jesus' name, I pray. Amen.

Prayer for Stepping Out in Faith

Faithful God,

You have called me to a life of faith, to step out into the unknown with confidence in Your promises. Today, I come before You, seeking Your guidance and courage as I take bold steps of faith.

Lord, I acknowledge that faith requires action. Help me to overcome fear and doubt, knowing that You are with me every step of the way. Grant me the strength to step out of my comfort zone and into the plans and purposes You have for my life.

Give me a heart that is sensitive to Your leading, Lord. Open my ears to hear Your voice and my eyes to see the opportunities You place before me. Help me to discern Your will and align my actions with Your desires.

Lord, when obstacles arise or when the path seems uncertain, empower me to trust in Your provision and guidance. Remind me that You are the God of miracles, and nothing is impossible with You. Increase my faith to believe that You will make a way where there seems to be no way.

Grant me a spirit of obedience, Lord. Help me to surrender my own plans and desires to You, being willing to go wherever You lead and do whatever You ask of me. Strengthen me to persevere in the face of challenges and to remain steadfast in my commitment to follow You.

Lord, I confess that I cannot walk this journey of faith alone. Surround me with a community of believers who will support and encourage me. Help me to build relationships with those who will spur me on in my faith and challenge me to step out even further.

Thank You, Lord, for the privilege of living a life of faith. Help me to embrace each day as an opportunity to walk hand in hand with You, trusting in Your guidance and provision. May my life be a testament to the transformative power of faith in You.

In Jesus' name, I pray. Amen.

Chapter 8: Nurturing Self-Compassion

Prayer for Self-Acceptance and Love

Loving Father,

I come before You with a humble heart, recognizing my need for self-acceptance and love. Help me to see myself through Your eyes, as a cherished and beloved child. Grant me the grace to embrace my true identity in You.

Lord, I confess that I often struggle with self-criticism and feelings of inadequacy. I compare myself to others and allow negative thoughts to consume my mind. Today, I surrender these burdens to You and ask for Your healing touch.

Fill me with the understanding of Your unconditional love and acceptance. Help me to believe that I am fearfully and wonderfully made, with unique gifts and talents that You have bestowed upon me. Free me from the need to seek validation from others and teach me to find my worth in You alone.

Lord, release me from the chains of perfectionism and self-doubt. Grant me the strength to let go of unrealistic expectations and to embrace my imperfections. Help me to see them as opportunities for growth and learning, rather than as sources of shame or failure.

Teach me to love and care for myself as You love and care for me. Show me how to extend the same grace, forgiveness, and compassion to myself that You extend to me daily. Help me to treat myself with kindness and gentleness, knowing that I am a precious creation of Yours.

Lord, transform my inner dialogue. Replace self-condemnation with words of affirmation and encouragement. Help me to cultivate a mindset of self-compassion, where I offer myself grace and forgiveness, just as You have offered it to me.

Thank You, Lord, for Your unconditional love and

acceptance. Help me to love myself as You love me. May my life reflect the beauty of self-acceptance, and may it inspire others to embrace their true worth in You.

In Jesus' name, I pray. Amen.

Prayer for Healing Inner Wounds

Compassionate Healer,

I come before You, recognizing the wounds and hurts that reside deep within my soul. I acknowledge the pain and brokenness that I carry, and I invite Your healing presence into those wounded places.

Lord, I surrender to You the scars of past hurts, disappointments, and betrayals. I ask for Your divine touch to bring healing and restoration to those wounded areas of my heart. Heal the wounds that have caused me to doubt my worth, to fear vulnerability, and to struggle with trusting others.

Pour out Your love and grace upon me, Lord, as You gently mend the broken pieces of my soul. Help me to release bitterness, resentment, and unforgiveness, knowing that they only hinder my own healing and growth. Grant me the courage to forgive those who have hurt me, just as You have forgiven me.

Lord, I invite You to speak words of truth and affirmation into the depths of my being. Replace the lies and negative self-perceptions with Your words of love, acceptance, and purpose. Help me to see myself through Your eyes, as a beloved child who is worthy of love and capable of healing.

Grant me the strength and wisdom to seek help and support in my healing journey. Surround me with compassionate individuals who can offer guidance, encouragement, and wise counsel. Help me to find healing in community, as I share my struggles and journey toward wholeness.

Lord, I surrender my pain and brokenness to You. Fill me with Your peace that surpasses all understanding. May Your healing touch restore my joy, renew my hope, and transform me from the inside out.

Thank You, Lord, for Your promise of healing and restoration. I trust in Your faithfulness, knowing that You are the Divine Physician who brings healing to the deepest parts of my being. I place my trust in Your loving care, knowing that You are able to bring beauty from ashes and turn my pain into purpose.

Prayer for Embracing God's Grace

Gracious God,

Your grace is abundant and unending, freely offered to all who seek it. Today, I come before You with a heart open to receive Your amazing grace. Help me to fully embrace and understand the depth of Your grace in my life.

Lord, I confess that I often struggle to accept Your grace. I carry the weight of my mistakes, shortcomings, and sins, allowing guilt and shame to burden my soul. Today, I release these heavy burdens to You and invite Your grace to wash over me.

Help me to comprehend the magnitude of Your love and mercy. Open my eyes to see that Your grace is not dependent on my performance or worthiness, but on Your unwavering love for me. Teach me to receive Your grace with humility and gratitude.

Lord, remind me that Your grace is sufficient for me. Help me to let go of self-condemnation and to trust in Your forgiveness. Grant me the strength to forgive myself and to extend grace to others, just as You have extended grace to me.

Guide me in living a life that reflects Your grace. Help me to extend compassion, kindness, and forgiveness to those around me. Show me how to be a vessel of Your grace, offering love and acceptance to others who are in need.

Lord, empower me to walk in freedom, liberated from the chains of guilt and shame. Help me to step into the fullness of life that Your grace provides. Give me the courage to embrace new beginnings, to learn from my mistakes, and to grow in Your grace.

Thank You, Lord, for the gift of Your grace. May it transform me from the inside out, renewing my spirit and guiding me on the path of righteousness. May Your grace shine through me, drawing others to experience the boundless love and mercy found in You.

In Jesus' name, I pray. Amen.

Chapter 9: Growing in Spiritual Depth

Prayer for Spiritual Growth and Transformation

Heavenly Father,

I come before You with a longing in my heart to grow deeper in my relationship with You. I desire to experience spiritual growth and transformation in every aspect of my life. Open my heart and mind to Your presence and work within me.

Lord, I surrender my will and my desires to You, knowing that You have a perfect plan for my spiritual journey. Grant me the humility to recognize my need for growth and the willingness to be transformed by Your Spirit. Mold me into the person You have called me to be.

Guide me in the study of Your Word, Lord. Help me

to dig deeper into the treasures of Scripture, that I may gain wisdom, insight, and understanding. Speak to me through Your Word, illuminating truth and revealing Your heart to me. May Your Word be a lamp unto my feet and a light unto my path.

Lord, I long for a vibrant prayer life that connects me intimately with You. Teach me to pray with fervency and faith, pouring out my heart before You. Help me to listen for Your voice, to discern Your leading, and to align my desires with Your will. Strengthen my prayer life, that I may experience the power of communion with You.

Surround me with a community of believers who will challenge, encourage, and inspire me in my spiritual journey. Give me the humility to learn from others, the grace to extend forgiveness and grace, and the boldness to share my faith with others. Help me to grow in unity and love with my brothers and sisters in Christ.

Lord, grant me a hunger and thirst for righteousness. Help me to pursue holiness and live a life that honors You. Remove anything that hinders my spiritual growth and draw me closer to You. Fill me with Your Spirit, empowering me to live a life that reflects Your love, grace, and truth.

Thank You, Lord, for the privilege of growing in spiritual depth. May my journey of transformation inspire others to seek You wholeheartedly. May I continually be transformed by Your Spirit and become a vessel of Your love and light in this world.

In Jesus' name, I pray. Amen.

Prayer for Communion with God

Gracious God,

I come before You with a longing to experience deep communion with You. I desire to draw near to Your presence and to know You intimately. Help me to cultivate a vibrant and intimate relationship with You.

Lord, I recognize that You are a God who desires to be known and who invites me into a personal relationship with You. Grant me the grace to set aside distractions, busyness, and worldly pursuits, that I may prioritize time with You. Help me to create space in my life to seek Your face and to listen to Your voice.

Teach me the discipline of silence and solitude, Lord. In the quiet moments, enable me to quiet my mind, to still my heart, and to be fully present with You.

Remove any hindrances that prevent me from experiencing the depth of intimacy that You offer.

Lord, help me to approach You with reverence and awe. May my worship be genuine and my prayers heartfelt. Teach me to pour out my praise and thanksgiving before You, acknowledging Your goodness, faithfulness, and love. May my worship draw me closer to You and deepen our connection.

Grant me a spirit of discernment, Lord. Help me to recognize Your voice among the many voices that surround me. Give me wisdom to discern Your will and guidance for my life. May I be attentive to Your promptings and obedient to Your leading.

Lord, I hunger for a deeper understanding of Your Word. Help me to study and meditate on Scripture with a receptive heart. Illuminate the truths hidden within Your Word and reveal to me the depths of Your wisdom and knowledge. May Your Word become alive in my heart, transforming my thoughts, actions, and attitudes.

Lord, I long to experience the fullness of Your presence. Help me to cultivate a spirit of surrender, laying down my own desires and agenda before You. Fill me with Your Holy Spirit, that I may be empowered to live a life that honors and glorifies You.

In the midst of the busyness and noise of this world, remind me to pause and seek Your face. Draw me into the depths of Your love, where I can find rest, peace, and renewal. Help me to abide in You, knowing that apart from You, I can do nothing.

Lord, I recognize that communion with You is not a one-sided endeavor. It requires me to listen, to be still, and to wait upon You. Teach me patience and trust as I wait upon Your perfect timing and Your divine guidance. Help me to surrender my own agendas and align my heart with Your purposes.

Thank You, Lord, for the invitation to draw closer to You. May my pursuit of communion with You be marked by authenticity, humility, and a deep hunger for Your presence. Transform me through our intimate communion, that I may reflect Your love and grace to the world around me.

In Jesus' name, I pray. Amen.

Prayer for Drawing Closer to Christ

Loving Savior,

I come before You with a desire to draw closer to You, to know You more intimately, and to follow You wholeheartedly. Help me to deepen my relationship with You and to become more like You in every aspect of my life.

Lord, I confess that at times I have allowed the distractions and busyness of life to pull me away from You. Today, I commit to making You the center of my life, the One to whom I turn for guidance, strength, and purpose. Renew my passion for You and ignite a fire within me to follow You with unwavering devotion.

Grant me a heart of humility, Lord, that I may submit to Your lordship in all areas of my life. Show me any areas where I have held back and give me the courage to surrender them to You. Help me to lay down my own desires and ambitions, that Your will may be done in and through me.

Lord, teach me to walk in obedience to Your Word. Open my eyes to the truths and principles found in Scripture. Give me the grace to live out Your teachings and to follow Your example of love, compassion, and selflessness. Help me to be a faithful disciple, reflecting Your character and sharing Your gospel with others.

Fill me with a hunger and thirst for righteousness, Lord. Transform my heart, my thoughts, and my attitudes to align with Your truth. Remove anything that hinders my intimacy with You and replace it with a deep longing to know You more.

Draw me closer to You through prayer, Lord. Help me to cultivate a consistent and fervent prayer life, where I can pour out my heart to You, listen to Your voice, and experience the joy of communion with You. Teach me to rely on Your strength, wisdom, and guidance in every aspect of my life.

Thank You, Lord, for Your unfailing love and grace. As I draw closer to You, may Your presence permeate every area of my life. May my relationship with You deepen and transform me into a faithful follower, reflecting Your love and light to a world in need.

In the precious name of Jesus, I pray. Amen.

CONCLUSION

Embracing Personal Growth and Transformation

As we come to the end of this prayer book, we reflect upon the journey of personal growth and transformation that we have embarked upon together. Throughout these chapters, we have explored various areas of our lives where we seek growth, renewal, and alignment with God's will. We have approached these areas with open hearts, seeking God's guidance, and offering prayers of surrender, healing, and empowerment.

Embracing personal growth and transformation is a lifelong journey. It requires humility, intentionality, and a deep reliance on God's grace and transforming power. It is not always an easy path, but it is a path that leads to abundant life, purpose, and a deeper connection with our Creator.

Through our prayers, we have acknowledged our need for God's strength in times of change, our dependence on Him in overcoming challenges, and our desire for inner transformation. We have sought His guidance, wisdom, and discernment as we discover and utilize our gifts and talents. We have surrendered our lives to His purposes, embraced self-compassion, and deepened our faith and trust in Him. We have nurtured a meaningful life, cultivated communion with God, and grown in spiritual depth. Throughout this journey, we have been blessed by His grace, and we have experienced the transformative power of His love.

As we conclude this book, let us remember that personal growth and transformation do not end here. They are ongoing processes that continue throughout our lives. May the prayers and reflections within these pages serve as a foundation for your ongoing journey of growth and transformation.

Final Prayer of Blessing

Gracious God,

We come before You with hearts full of gratitude for the journey we have shared in this prayer book. We thank You for the privilege of seeking personal growth and transformation in Your presence. We acknowledge that without You, we are nothing, but with You, all things are possible.

Lord, as we close this book, we ask for Your continued guidance and presence in our lives. May the prayers we have offered be seeds that take root in our hearts and bear abundant fruit. Grant us the strength to persevere in times of change, the peace to navigate challenges, and the courage to step out in faith.

Bless us, Lord, with a renewed sense of purpose and meaning. May our gifts and talents be used to glorify You and serve others. Grant us the wisdom to discern Your will and the openness to follow Your direction.

Continue to transform us from the inside out, Lord. Heal our wounds, restore our souls, and renew our minds. Help us to extend grace and compassion to ourselves and others, reflecting Your love and forgiveness.

Deepen our relationship with You, Lord. Draw us closer to Your heart and help us to abide in Your presence. May our communion with You be a source of strength, guidance, and deep joy.

Strengthen our faith and trust in You, Lord. Help

us to walk boldly in Your ways, to trust Your timing, and to surrender our lives to Your divine plan. May our lives be a testament to Your faithfulness and goodness.

As we continue to grow in spiritual depth, Lord, shape us into vessels of Your love and instruments of Your peace. May our lives reflect Your character, shining Your light in a world that desperately needs it.

We conclude this prayer book with hearts full of gratitude, knowing that the journey of personal growth and transformation is ongoing. We thank You, Lord, for the work You have done and will continue to do in our lives.

In Jesus' name, we pray. Amen.

May you embrace personal growth and transformation with a steadfast heart, knowing that God is with you every step of the way. May His love, grace, and power bring forth the fullness of your potential and enable you to live a life that honors Him. May you continually seek His guidance, trust in His plan, and surrender to His will. May the prayers in this book be a source of inspiration, encouragement, and empowerment as you navigate the journey of personal growth and transformation.

Remember, that you are fearfully and wonderfully made by a loving Creator. He has placed within you unique gifts, talents, and a divine purpose. Embrace the opportunities for growth and transformation that come your way, knowing that God is equipping you for His good work.

As you step forward on this journey, may you approach each day with a heart of gratitude and a spirit of humility. Seek wisdom and understanding through prayer, study of God's Word, and fellowship with other believers. Surround yourself with a community of support, accountability, and encouragement.

Be patient with yourself, for personal growth takes time. Celebrate the progress you make, no matter how small it may seem, and trust that God is at work in every step of your journey. He is faithful to complete the good work He has begun in you.

May your pursuit of personal growth and transformation be rooted in love—for God, for yourself, and for others. May your life be a living testimony of God's grace and redemption. And may the fruit of your growth and transformation impact the world around you, drawing others closer to the heart of God.

May the blessings of personal growth and transformation be upon you. May you walk confidently in the path that God has set before you, knowing that He is with you every step of the way. May you continually seek His face, surrender to His will, and experience the abundant life He has prepared for you.

May your life be a reflection of His love, a testament to His power, and a source of inspiration to those around you. And may you find joy, fulfillment, and purpose as you embrace personal growth and transformation in the embrace of our loving Heavenly Father.

In the name of Jesus, our Redeemer and Friend, we pray. Amen.